Special
Friends
Words and Pictures by
Karen Vanderlaan
AF583148
Chrysalis
BALM AND BLADE PUBLISHING

ISBN: 978-1-961261-02-0

Published by Chrysalis / Balm and Blade Publishing
1927 Mountain Road, Hamburg, PA 19526
www.balmandblade.com

Interior layout & design by Jason Vanderlaan

Dedicated to Elyssa and Crystal

Under the Moon, a late-night ride,
Set to the sweet music of you;
Singing, "Twinkle, Twinkle, Little Star,"
You and your pony on a ride in the dark.

I had one arm around you,
The other held the rope.
Crystal's feet were sure,
Her eyes, wise from many such children's rides.

You rode around and around the farm,
Calling out the name of every horse as we passed.
"Hi Tribute and Angel, I'm riding Crystal."
"Trot Crystal, trot slow. Elyssa doesn't want to fall."

Crystal is a very small pony. She lived for many years with her family. Crystal taught the family's children to ride and had four babies of her own.

All the children have now grown up and Crystal has grown old. Crystal could not take care of herself very well. She is very thin. Crystal needs to go to a new home where she can be taken care of.

Crystal's new home is a small horse farm. Elyssa's grandma lives there, and she takes care of all the horses who live there. Elyssa is very young and very small. She loves all the big horses on the farm but Crystal is just her size.

Crystal needs special food because most of her teeth are gone. Elyssa climbs into Crystal's pen and says, "It's okay, Crystal, it's me, Elyssa. I will feed you your dinner."

Crystal goes to Elyssa, who feeds her the soft food with a big wooden spoon.

There is a lot more to loving a pony than most people think. Elyssa watches as her grandma takes care of the big horses. Elyssa is too small to help. Crystal is small and gentle. Elyssa cleans her stall.

It took a few trips back and forth, but Elyssa can carry the right amount of hay for Crystal.

A pony needs to be brushed every day so they can be comfortable. Elyssa can brush Crystal all by herself. She brushes all the dirt off of Crystal, even reaching her nose!

Crystal's feet also need care. Elyssa cleans them all by herself. Crystal is always careful not to move.

Crystal's back holds Elyssa perfectly. It is just the right distance from the ground for Elyssa to feel safe. Elyssa rides all over the farm.

Crystal always listens to Elyssa's voice as she tells her to walk, trot, and canter. "Canter really slow. Elyssa doesn't want to fall off." Crystal listens. She always canters really slow.

Sometimes, Elyssa pretends she is a beautiful princess on a magical white pony.

Other times, Elyssa practices her posting.
"Up – down, up – down."

After their ride, Crystal needs a cool shower. Elyssa loves to squirt her with the hose. Sometimes, Elyssa gets as wet as Crystal.

For Crystal and Elyssa, the days on the farm are full of sunshine and friendship.

# Also available from Karen Vanderlaan:

The name of the horse in this book comes from the Old Testament in the Bible. As a young teen I was sitting in church, flipping through my Bible. I came across the name Chenaniah in First Chronicles. Chenaniah was a chief musician. I decided to name my new horse, Chenaniah. The 'ch' is pronounced 'sh' as in ship. I called him Chen for short. My mother bought him when I was 15 and I worked the summer I turned 16 to buy him from her. I had fallen in love with him from the moment I first saw him. He was my dream horse, my Earthly Pegasus. When I moved, he moved with me, and when I had my daughter, she formed a very special bond with him. This is their little story.

www.ingramcontent.com/pod-product-compliance
Lightning Source LLC
LaVergne TN
LVHW071227160826
845679LV00003B/928
* 9 7 8 1 9 6 1 2 6 1 0 2 0 *